KU-436-499

TONGUES OF FIRE

BY THE SAME AUTHOR

NON-FICTION

J.M. Synge: Nature, Politics, Modernism

TONGUES OF FIRE

Seán Hewitt

CAPE POETRY

3 5 7 9 10 8 6 4 2

Jonathan Cape, an imprint of Vintage,
20 Vauxhall Bridge Road,
London SW1V 2SA

Jonathan Cape is part of the Penguin Random House group of companies
whose addresses can be found at global.penguinrandomhouse.com

Copyright © Seán Hewitt 2020

Seán Hewitt has asserted his right to be identified as the
author of this Work in accordance with the Copyright, Designs
and Patents Act 1988

First published by Jonathan Cape in 2020

penguin.co.uk/vintage

A CIP catalogue record for this book is available
from the British Library

ISBN 9781787332263

Typeset in 11/13 pt Bembo by Jouve (UK), Milton Keynes
Printed and bound in Great Britain by TJ International Ltd, Padstow, Cornwall

Penguin Random House is committed to a sustainable future for
our business, our readers and our planet. This book is made
from Forest Stewardship Council® certified paper.

for my parents

CONTENTS

LEAF

For woods are forms of grief
grown from the earth. For they creak

with the weight of it.
For each tree is an altar to time.

For the oak, whose every knot
guards a hushed cymbal of water.

For how the silver water holds
the heavens in its eye.

For the axletree of heaven
and the sleeping coil of wind

and the moon keeping watch.
For how each leaf traps light as it falls.

For even in the nighttime of life
it is worth living, just to hold it.

BARN OWLS IN SUFFOLK

I watch them for a long while,
the pair rising and courting the field
in daylight, the strange geometry
of their faces funneling the air,

and everything – their whiteness,
their sense of having slipped
through from another world,
their focus on the hunt –

in the end it all comes down
to their silence –
the way each feather disperses
the air, how each wavers –

and I wonder what omen it is
to see two barn owls hunting
in mid-morning, so quietly
secretive, for surely

there is something in the slow
spread of the wing, the moment
of inverted flight, the living thing
pulled from the earth and lifted.

DRYAD

I remember her covered in snow in a field
where each dead stalk of wildflower was thick
with frost. The sky was pink in the hawthorns,

the day held on the light-edge of breaking.
A woman carved from the bole of an oak,
her feet (if she had any) buried in the winter's

shedding weight. Whoever had turned her
from the tree had given her an orb
which she held in both hands, close to the gentle

curve of her face. And she stood there
by the half-rotten stile off Broad Lane,
head bowed, as though waiting to greet us

and offer the frozen circumference of a new
world. Years ago, our school had planted
the woods behind her, when I was eight or nine,

and now each tree ages alongside us.
Every time I go back, I see a part
of my life laid out, still growing in a field

by the old village. I used to come here
often, at eighteen or so, with men at night
and it was strange to pass her as we stumbled

in the undergrowth and into the woods
like deer plummeting through the wet branches.
And I think now of all the men forced outside

after clearing-out, into the dark spaces of towns,
how they walk in vigil to woodlands and old
estates, to the smell of the day settling. Once,

I came here with a man whose whole body
was muscled, as though he too had been carved
from a single trunk of wood. I pretended

all the time to be a man like him,
answering each lie in a deep, alien voice.
I think I was afraid he would kill me,

and walked a few steps ahead, hearing
him moving through the sodden grass,
pulling his feet from the bramble-vines.

We passed the woman without comment,
though she stood there in her cloak of wood,
the globe held in the lathed green of her hands.

Here was so unlike the places other people went,
a place without doors or walls or rooms.
The black heavy-leafed branches pulled back

like a curtain and inside a dark chamber
of the wood, guarded, and made safe.
The bed was the bed of all the plants

and trees, and we could share it. And then
the kneeling down in front of him, keeping
my secrets still in the folds of night, trying

not to shake in the cold, and the damp floor
seeping up. I remember the cold water
spreading in the capillaries of my jeans.

As I looked up, the sky hidden under a rain
of leaves, each tree stood over me
in perfect symmetry with his body.

Each was like a man with his head bent,
each watching and moving and making slow
laboured sighs. I came back often,

year on year, kneeling and being knelt for
in acts of secret worship, and now
each woodland smells quietly of sex,

not only when the air is thick with it,
but in winter too when the strains
are grounded and held against the earth,

and each time I half-expect
to meet someone among the trees
or inside the empty skeleton

of the rhododendron, and I wonder if I have ruined
these places for myself, if I have brought
each secret to them and weighed the trees

with things I can no longer bear. But then
what is a tree, or a plant, if not an act
of kneeling to the earth, a way of bidding

the water to move, of taking in the mouth
the inner part of the world and coaxing it out.
Not just the aching leaf-buds

in spring, the cloud of pollen, or in autumn
the children knocking branches for the shower
of seed, but the people who kneel in the woods

at night, the woman waiting by the gate, offering
to each visitor a small portion of the world
in which they might work for the life of it.

HÄCKSJÖN

running barefoot, green moss lit
between trees, I go one foot after
the other, arriving on instinct
between roots, dodging

with white feet the white slugs
swelled on forestlight, and you
disappear ahead of slanting pines –
my pale step padding on this sloping

peat path that sinks like a trapdoor
underfoot, and then I leap . . . I love
to plunge through the black glass
of the lake, to make it echo

with my body, feeling the water's
cold resistance . . . for a long moment
I plumb its dark core, and then its arms
rush in and lift me back to the light.

KYRIE

Purple blush of sky and lilac drooping
by the greenhouse. The last heat of day
rests in the grass, and from the shadows
under the conifers, there comes a moaning,

a pain riddling from the undergrowth,
a voice caught out after dark. And my mind,
closed off from sight and the body's reading
of the world, convinces me it is the crying

of a child left out in the yard behind ours.
Naked, its soft fat limbs and wet mouth open
and wailing and helpless. I stand frozen
by the back door and the quiet house,

trying to listen, receptive but distrusting
my body — the ring of light from the kitchen
over my shoulder making the garden
a more solid darkness beyond the patio,

like the darkness that lives behind eyelids.
I swear at first the crying seems to stop
my heart as I think of it, sends my mind
whirring outwards into the night. Trance-like,

I begin to move further from the light
of the window, slow enough
for my eyes to reinterpret with each step
the shapes of bushes, the forms of shirts

hanging on the line, but still I cannot imagine
the sound as anything but a child cursing
in the pitch-dark conifers. As I walk closer,
my hands white in the garden air, a sudden

panic breaks in the bushes, a brawling,
and I see the darker shapes of two cats
mating. It is here, by the swaying trees,
away from the glow of the house,

that I realise I have found myself at a place
so close to life, to its truth of violence,
that my mind has wired out, but even now
I could not say which was the truer thought:

the cats or the lost child; and I think again
of calling home that night from Sweden,
of hearing my mother's voice and telling her
what you had done (tablets, rum, calling

to say goodbye), and how I made
an animal sound, a noise so primitive
that I felt inhuman, how I cried
like something new-born

because I had found myself
in a world where all abstract things
(death, fear, loss) had bloomed in my mind,
and what is a parent to a child but a god

who we turn to when we still believe
that everything is fixable, a god
who we weep to as we grow
into the world, as we age into it

and each abstraction comes closer.
And now I am back in the garden,
staring into the conifers, the kitchen light
receding from my shoulders,

and considering all the ways
a mind can uproot itself,
all the short-circuits left in the world.
I am thinking of the shadows

under trees, the lives of animals,
the places where words extinguish
themselves and leave all the things
that cannot be fixed or forgotten.

ST JOHN'S WORT

Named for a man who carries his own head
on a platter, for a day when the sun bears
its light over the land so slowly, so measuredly,
that the night crouches back and waits. A token
of love, of patience, of the will to lift the mind
outside oneself, and let it rest. Let it heal. Alone,
I remembered this little herb, the yellow spikes
of the flower, frill of stamen, as something akin
to happiness − its bright stars, its tiny play
at hope, its way of lifting through the grass −
and I brought it to you, a light to illumine
the dark caves of your eyes. At the door
of the ward, being searched, the nurse
took from me my gathering of flowers.
I found you on the bed, staring, still in shock.
Bringing no gift, I took your head
in my empty hands like a world and held it.

HÄRSKOGEN

Each night I would drive this way:
the beam of the headlights tracking
over the effigies of pines, the radio
threatening to falter with each
deepening turn. The lane was long,
lined with rows of towering fir, higher
than any hope of star or half-spent
moon. A lost city, a mind unmoving
in its meditation, the deer left to walk
their shadows among the trees.

Each night, leaving you
in the hospital, I dared myself
to pull over, to switch the engine off.
The cold air would hold me, beating,
in its tourniquet, and the mist would sink
and lift untethered through the beams.
Then, one by one, each tree
would take focus: the cracked age
of the lower bark, violence of the snapped
branch-crown. Everything was silenced

by the endless stretching upwards, life
lifted a little further over my head.
Behind this tree, many hundreds more
of equal size and strength, and the lakes
freezing gradually in the dells. But here,
only this pine, this circle of trees, one of many
quiet circles. And I would stand thinking
of you, smelling the sap well up from the wounds
and watching the mist, like an old dog,
trying over and over to settle at my feet.

DORMANCY

Delicate, grown old in its separation,
a wych elm can send itself to seed –
can sow from its body these translucent

frailties. Like hanging wombs –
ghosts of seed speaking
in their dried-out bristle of tree-skin.

Just so, visiting you on the ward
where death had been taken, locked
into the matron's safe. You who knew

how separate a person is, how deep
a root can search into darkness
unobstructed. After seeing you

so sexless, unable, I sowed myself
like a wych elm in a windless room.

OAK GLOSSARY

In the language of the oak, *sky*
is made by shivering the leaves
to produce a hushing sound.
In winter, of course, *sky* is silent.

God is felt in the phloem and xylem
as a deep echo of water – a low noise
that must be observed by placing
an ear to the bark. For oaks, *chanting*

(which is akin to *song*) is produced
via rhythms of air brought in and out
of the branches in slow succession.
On still days, *song* is not possible.

The familiar words, such as *child*,
man, *woman*, are unknown, having
fallen quiet from disuse. In oak,
essential nouns include *soil*,

water and *time* – these are produced
from their elements. *Water* is a high
and gentle noise of clearest quality
which results from branches dripping.

For *soil*, or *earth*, a fastening of the roots
can be felt as a low tension underfoot.
Time, on the other hand, is more visual
than aural, and is distinguished into

its linear and circular conceptions.
As is well-known, *circular time*
in oak is communicated
most vividly at the site of a knot

or where the core has been exposed.
The linear variety is felt only
on occasion. For this, sap is produced
and is made to run from the body.

PSALM

Now the earth is tilted
on the edge of night, I walk out
with my lantern like the messenger

of God. The fog wraps
the branches: ghost of field hangs
over the field, a drowned man

in pearls weeps under a bridge.
To each, I confess a secret.

Same weather last year, a glitch
in the workings, was the night
you took yourself to the water

and knelt. In white breath,
*for the waters are come
unto my soul.* Since then

a lifted hinge in the mind
and life came loose.
                    Now, from the fog,

time's small currency: iron coins,
iron water.

From the fog: coated horses, marsh-
grass; wings, fence-posts, the long
suffering bodies of trees.

CLOCK

A close warm evening opened by rain –
and me (caught out) leaning on a cedar.

A heron walks its white zed
along the bank and out into the water,

and just here a small beetle, sheen
of coal-black, pulls itself into the pink bed

of the rhododendron flower. Then, once
and once more, a fox barks –

and, though I love you and I know
there is no such thing as held time,

this tree seems suddenly like a stillness,
a circle of quiet air, a place to stand

now that I have had to leave
and cannot think where I might go next.

WILD GARLIC

Out in the copse after rain
(too late after dark to be here).
Warm soil, woodlice dripping
from the underside of leaves.

I root down to the tender stalks
and twist them free – soaked petals
dip and touch my arm, kernels
of bud, itch of foliage, of wildness

on my skin. The plants are carrying
the smell, earth-rich, too heavy
to lift above head-height, and my boots
and jeans are bleached with it.

I turn home, and all across the floor
the spiked white flowers
light the way. The world is dark
but the wood is full of stars.

from
BUILE SUIBHNE

SUIBHNE IN THE GLEN

After Suibhne was cursed, he wandered Ireland
for weeks, searching in the cavities of rocks
and roots, climbing the ivy-strung trees and peering
over the canopies until he found Glen Bolcain.

This was where all the madmen came. Here,
the little wood was dotted with sturdy wells
and clear, sand-flanked streams covered
in watercress, and the brooklime leaning over.

The wood was full of oaks, wood-sorrels,
garlic, blackthorns and trees whose names
were lost between the lips of men. Naked,
Suibhne walked its soft paths and slept

high in a hawthorn on the glen's slope.
At night, each twist and turn of his dream
would set the thorns into his body, and soon
his limbs were cut and swollen. After that

he chose another place — a thicket of bramble
where the thorns were finer, and a single
white-blossomed arm of blackthorn sheltered
the plants from the rain. Even though his body

was frail, with his white skin stretched tight
over the ribs and his collarbones sticking out,
the little blackthorn gave way one night
under his weight. He thought, it is hard to live

without a home. It is hard to be a whole year
under the gloom of branches. It is hard
to be without the sound of children
or music or the voices of women,

and it is cold, cold for me now —
since my body has lived outside
much rain has fallen upon it
and much thunder.

SUIBHNE VISITS EORANN

During this time, Suibhne's wife, Eorann, was living with Guaire. One day, Guaire had been hunting, riding through the pass of Sliabh Fuaid and by Sgirig Cinn Glinne and Ettan Tairbh, and his camp was by Glen Bolcain. Suibhne came down to the camp, and sat up on the lintel of the hut where his wife was staying. He said, 'I wonder if you remember the love we used to pass to each other when we were together, Eorann? Things have worked out well for you, it seems; though it has not been so easy for me.' And she spoke kindly to him, telling how her body was wasting since he left, and how, to her, he was the most welcome man on earth. And she said,

> Even if the prince himself led me
> through halls banked with riches,
> I'd rather sleep in a dark tree-hollow
> with you, my husband, if you'd let me.

> If all the men of Ireland and of Scotland
> stood undressed in a line before me,
> I'd choose to stay here with you
> and live on water and on watercress.

SUIBHNE DREAMS OF EORANN

black arrowheads
shimmering, repeating
in waves, crashing, turning,

the world spins
above our heads
but nothing drops,

nothing falls but a delicate
rain of leaf shaken wild
over our little globe

SUIBHNE ESCAPES, AND IS SET WANDERING

No matter where I go
my sins follow. First,
the starry frost will fall
at night onto every pool,
and me left out in it, straying

on the mountain. And then
the herons will be crying
in the cold of Glen Aighle,
and the flocks of birds
will be leaving overhead.

I live with the frost, sleep
in its bed, have for pillow
the rough, wind-driven snow.
And when the skylarks come

I hide from them, shaking,
shelter by a single oak
until the weak sun kindles
and I must stumble again

from the old tree-top,
and leave once more
by the deer-paths
over the red field.

SUIBHNE GOES OVER
THE SEA TO BRITAIN, AND
MEETS FER CAILLE

When Suibhne left Carraig Alastair he went over the open-mouthed, storm-battered sea until he reached the land of the Britons. There he passed by a great wood, and as he passed he heard a loud lamenting and sighing and wailing, a great weep of sadness and a small moan of sorrow, and he found another madman wandering amongst the trees. He approached slowly, with caution, and asked the man who he was, and they told each other their tales. And the man, happy to have found a friend like himself, sang to Suibhne:

> O Suibhne, let's keep guard
> over each other, now
> that we have found ourselves.
> Whoever hears the heron cry
>
> from the crystal lake,
> or the clear call of the cormorant,
> or the clap of the woodcock
> from the branch, or the whoop
>
> of a plover woken from its sleep,
> or the sound of branches snapping;
> whoever first feels the cold of a bird's
> shadow passing overhead, let him
>
> tell the other, let us care
> for each other. Let us never sleep
> more than two trees apart
> for the whole length of the year.

And they did so, and lived happily, and after a year had turned between them, they each told the other how they were to die, and it was time for Fer Caille to meet his end under the weight of a waterfall, and so with mournful tears and sweet tears they parted, and Suibhne returned to Ireland.

And when Suibhne returned, his mind was healed, and he went in search of his kin.

Ronan heard about this, and prayed to the Lord that there should be no respite for Suibhne, and his prayer was answered. And so when Suibhne came to Sliabh Fuaid, he stopped in his tracks, and a strange apparition appeared to him at midnight: five red heads without bodies on the edge of the wood, each screaming in agony and shouting the words of his curse at Suibhne in deep unearthly voices until he cried and wept aloud and flew off from thicket to thicket, hill to hill, rushing and beating his arms until he could no longer hear those voices or see those terrible visions.

And after a long time passing from place to place, homeless and beaten down, Suibhne went to his friend, a cleric called Moling, where he was destined to end his wandering, and was pierced in the side with a spear.

SUIBHNE IS WOUNDED,
AND CONFESSES

There was a time when I thought
the sound of a dove cooing and flitting
over a pond was sweeter than the voices

of friends. There was a time when
I preferred the blackbird and the boom
of a stag belling in a storm. I used to think

that the chanting of the mountain-grouse
at dawn had more music than your voice,
but things are different now. Still,

it would be hard to say I wouldn't rather
live above the bright lake, and eat watercress
in the wood, and be away from sorrow.

Suibhne fainted then, and died, and Moling and the clerics rose, and each planted a stone over Suibhne's tomb. 'The one who lies here is dear indeed', Moling said. 'Often, in happy times, we two would walk together in conversation on this path. Every time I saw him, my heart would lift. But now his tomb is by this well – we'll call it the madman's well, for often he would eat its watercress and drink its water. Every place that Suibhne went is dear to me.' And then Moling said,

Glen Bolcain seems lovely to me
because Suibhne loved it,
and its clear, high streams
and its crop of watercress.

And here is the well of Suibhne,
my poor man. I love its water,
which slaked his thirst, and its sand,
and the bright plants it is holding.

Each talk with Suibhne was music
for me, and I will keep that tune
in my breast and hear it in the birds
of Glen Bolcain and in the singing

of this little stream, where the green
watercress grows and the bright
water dances, which is dear to me
because Suibhne used to come here.

GHOST

i.

Waking, close to morning but still
a shuttered, metal dark in the room:
a sound inside my dream, only a whimper
at first, then becoming human, a howl
raised in the street outside, left unanswered
then raised again. In my boxers, shivering
by the single-paned window, but seeing no one
among the black shapes of the parked cars
or hedges, I went out half-dressed: hands shaking,
front door unlocked then pushed open,
and by the column of the porch, under a cone
of orange light, a young man slumped,
drunk, sobbing like his whole life
was unfurling into sound.

ii.

And now, I am reminded of one afternoon,
home from school, my father digging out
the root of a conifer in the garden — I saw him
look up, suddenly alert, leave by the back gate
into the alley behind the terraces, and return
panicked with a boy in his arms. I recognised him,
about my age, from school, by his dreadlocks,
his turquoise streak of hair; but now lolling
under his own weight, his wrists draining
over my father's mudded jeans and the patio tiles.
I knew, even then, the rumours about him;
thought as we wrapped and pinned torn sheets
around his opened veins, how we might share,
once the truth was out, a bond, an elective blood.

iii.

Nights later, I only half-slept, expecting
at any moment to hear someone again outside,
as though time might be caught in a loop,
the same boy walking the mapped route
along the dark streets at the same hour
to my door. Again, I unshuttered the window,
stood waiting to see him come, barefoot, maybe,
down the path. Each night, no sign, until I thought,
perhaps, it was only me, or a dream of myself,
asking nightly to be greeted at the threshold,
allowed back into the cold room of my life.
But then, in each of us, a wound must be made
or given — there is always the soul waiting
at the door of the body, asking to be let out.

CALLERY PEAR

All of a sudden it stops me —
acrid and sour-white, wafting
in sheets as the pollen catches the sun

then billows upwards —
the same smell, loosing now
in drifts through the hot streets

and then, as I breathe, clenching
deep under my sacrum: a fist
of longing, call of silvered

nights when I would make
my body burst its bloom
then snug down, half-

sweated; the stain of myself
(smelling almost of another man)
held like blossom to my nose.

OCTOBER

Once, I knelt staring in a garden
in mid-autumn at the last
of the marrow flowers –

a pair pushed up out of nowhere
overnight, too late for the season:
one bent under dew, the frail skin

of the other already turning
slowly back to water.
And yet the leaves bristled

in the wind – the tired petals
not quite ready to give up
to the cold, though each

was a distillation of the sun's
late colour. And I saw myself
kneeling in the garden

from far away, caught between
one man I no longer love,
another I might never.

This is how the world turns:
love like a marrow flower closing,
like another trying still to open.

EVENING POEM

First the clatter-iron blackbird,
its fanatical shuddering in the magnolia.

Dusk, and the garden is re-assembling,
calling its sparrows home,

and what a voice-racket under the aucuba
(doors closing to) and each sparrow

an iron-filing sweeping the field-lines
of the garden. I sit out in the last warmth

and watch it all come to rest:
the light falling, the thrushes settling

in the sycamores at the far end
of the lawn, how each tree lowers itself

under a new weight, and I hold out
for a while for everything to darken,

for the birds to stop singing, as though
I am teaching myself again to bear it.

MOOR

is childless, sulks
speaks rain and sudden light

is a mind
is sleepless, lies deep in its bed
is always moving about at night

speaks fog with its moss-mouth
is turned to sea by the wind
is waves in the dark, crashing

is suddenly still
is a trembling of light on the tent
is a shudder of guy-ropes and a shadow passing
is kept awake by its conscience

is always waiting,
sounds like breathing, sounds like
it is carrying bodies at night
when no one is watching

is a swallower of sound
wants every night to reach up
and swallow the moon, swallow something

is a mouth
hides and is never caught
sits in the dark quietly and smiles

as the farmer walks out
again with his torch-beam
calling and calling a name

OLD CROGHAN MAN

'their nipples were cut, thus rendering them ineligible for kingship . . .
the suckling of a king's nipples was an important gesture of submission'
                                  Eamonn P. Kelly, 'An Archaeological
                                  Interpretation of Irish Iron Age Bog Bodies'

Only a torso now, the head
long-severed from the neck, pelvis
twisted off like a stubborn root.

Remember the worn jacket
of his body pressed
in the bog; above, the galaxies

of cotton-grass turned
inside-out, like little souls
among the eyebrights,

the stitchwort. No place
to leave a man alone.
And under each nipple

a deep incision, blade-width.
Even then, they needed boys
like me – to leave power

in our wake, to dip our heads
and take to the soft
pink mound. I would have felt,

then, the making of a king;
known God, through my lips,
entering the body.

The woods are the organ
of the wind. The wind puts its hand

over the forest's mouth.
Trees struggle for breath, then faint.

It is a wood – it doesn't speak
except to itself. Its eyes are knots in bark

and it is April, and it's moving.
I can hear the soft, transmuted

aches of growing and easing back
to form, the forest creaking awake

around me. Then nothing but mutterings –
the sun bending its neck to look through trees,

birds building houses from the open ribs
of bushes. My quick movements startle

the sleeping leaves. When I turn, things speak . . .
Now the wood swallows me into its heart,

pushing weather rings behind bark
in its old, megalith slowness. I hold still,

hearing nothing but the crackle
of my own ears opening.

It starts to rain. It rains. The still day
whispers with the feedback of dead leaves

like dust translating on the air's vinyl.
Hold your ear

to the ground: you can hear
the voices caught in the earth, chattering,

and the rain typing on puddles
and the wind wiping them clean.

ILEX

after the birth of my nephew

Distracting myself, waiting for news,
I walked until I saw this white cluster
of holly growing at the base of a tree,

the stems yellowed, the angled clutch
of leaves like a bleached coral, a pale
antler, almost medieval, like a relic

unearthing in the gloom of the wood.
Later, still the baby would not latch,
and I came back to this holly, unhardened

by the sun, unable to turn the light
into strength. May it keep its whiteness,
may it never learn the use of spikes;

or, in time, when a crown is made of it,
may the people approach one by one
to witness how a fragile thing is raised.

IN PRINCE'S PARK

The orb-weavers have been working
overnight: slings of web linking
the rowan leaves, a silk circuitry

in the fog. It is almost
as though I have woken up here,
have walked in my sleep

through the last white day
of October to meet someone
but, arriving, have forgotten who.

And still the wood is filling itself
with itself: the leaves falling down
to the other leaves, and every so often

at intervals a woodpecker
in repeated short bursts
shakes hold of the quiet –

its echo
ricocheting, knocking
at each tree for the unsuspecting

bright splint of life, asking
who is home   who is home
and then snatching it out.

EPITHALAMIUM

Almost velvet to the hand,
but underneath alive with woodlice.

A fungus blackened by nights of rain
and crouched here in the lower

trunk of an oak. All its shelves
are sinking – the spread of layers

like tar poured and set and now,
again, melting into the soil –

a war-burnt body, its skin blistered
and peeling back to the soft heart –

a tumour on the wood – and I can hardly
bear to touch it – shaking at first, then

stroking it, patting it, kneeling down
and suddenly the tears. Cold, hardened,

the life all dissipated, all over – and this,
I know, is your palm, upturned for mine.

Our parents, when we were young,
teased us, sang nuptial hymns. I did not

realise how far I had walked you
into my life, until your hand let go.

DECEMBER

I imagine winter returning as if woken from a dream,
clambering from the iced rabbit-hole of the field,
open-mouthed. The sound it makes coming home
knee-deep in the night. Its slow feet, the numb toes.

I listen for the pain in the white shins of the birches,
splinter-trees charred by cold, limbs creaking.
What is the sound of winter? Bark dropping wetly
beneath the laid-down lace of the snow.

And where does it go? To the scales of the fish
which are its sequins, to the frost-skin of the pond
where it grows itself, to the branches of the water
in which it sits, spinning its own white body.

VESTIGE

A sash window blooming with frost.
December morning, and ferns of it

unfurling upwards – white feathers
of ice, the ghost of a wing on the glass.

From the bed, under heavy linen,
we watched how slowly the structures

of water unend themselves. Now,
across the field, I see you crouching

in rapture by the slate urinals, *frosted
in graceful sprays*. Night, it seems,

has fingered each effusion into a tree
of white crystal. I hear your cry

leap, then echo. Inside me,
the water branches: the world

rings like a glass, and my body
rings in the world like a glass.

ADORATION

St Stephen's Day: home unsettled,
a rupture, and here the ruched
branch has turned itself outwards,

its soft bright innards held up
along the path. At first, a golden
lobe on the oak, leaking

in the mist – fungus, 'yellow
tremble', translucent and half-aglow
with its own light; then more

appearing as I walk. A strange thing
being birthed alone out here
on the edges of the town,

the slow year becoming flesh
in amniotic colour; its soft fruit
hung along the corridor of gorse,

and all the while a constant
systole and diastole in the fog
as though the whole wrecked world

were a heart, beating. I stand here
for a while, staring at this half-born
life oozing in the cold, come unstuck,

brought out too soon. Weeks ago,
in the concrete, sub-zero of Berlin,
we huddled on the scrubland

by Ostbahnhof, watched the sun dip,
the light shifting blue, all the streets sinking.
Then, a reprieve: into the club,

its vaulted columns, the steel bars
and long-stemmed lilies, and the heat
scouring our skin. The building

was organ-warm, pulsing:
inside, long passages of people,
deep sound rippling outwards

and somewhere near the core
a room of masks, apparatus of leather,
a censer of white menthol swung

and resting at eye-level.
In the cubicle, a white pill held up,
broken – the heart fluttering,

and then the music, a congregation
undoing their bodies over
and over into beaming shapes.

We found a hidden place, turned
ourselves outwards in the humid cell –
bloom and spirit unspooling.

Back here on the heath, running
last summer until our faces
burned, we stopped for breath

in the gorse-tunnel – how eerie
it was at dusk, some dimension
we'd slipped into by chance.

I sprinted off into the dark
and you bolted to catch me,
held a blackberry to my mouth –

the sudden tang of it – plucked
too soon. My body winced
and smarted into colour, the day

distilled then taken gloriously
inside – host of the world –
and then a kiss – something

soft and secret and unseen. I know
I would kneel to you – blood, yes,
spine, lips. Leave me always

in these waste spaces, where
my head is tilted up to God
and I am a wild thing, glowing.

LAPWINGS

A March sky pinned with stars –
purple, almost, and a blue mist in the wheat-stubble.
Under the laburnum, we waited –
the chains of leaf, its cascades of gold flower
gone, and the whole tree drooping
like an open hand, loose at the wrist.
And in the far field – what?
The dun mare wickering, shifting
her weight; the trough half-frosted
and glittering. This might be

the last year, we thought, before the land
was sold; the nests with their four pointed eggs
in the scrape, the square plot peaked,
all those mothers, and who knows what else
before the year was out?
What losses? Until, near the tracks, a spark –
a dark firework lit in a flickering note
and us hushed to hear it, to follow the jet
of its firing, its leap up
and then the tumbling

fall: black sparks, the shower
of embers gashed and the catherine-wheel
flourish as the sound was dropped,
caught, then dashed to earth.
And what of it?
All beyond night's blind –
hardly even a shadow, but the air
just then, picked up, shaken to static –
cheee-o-wit of something like life whipping upwards
and the dying nerve shot along the bright rod of the spine.

EVENING POEM

What a world of apparitions:
stifled warmth of the greenhouse,
scent of tomatoes, my mother
and I working closely

to shimmy the pots
loose. Split sack of soil
on the bench, glow
of a tealight in the jar,

and not a word between us.
It is hard to tell where heaven
starts, and where it ends:
me, a foot taller, standing

where her father stood,
and outside, look: the dove,
like a paper lantern, is bobbing
in the apple-blossom.

PETITION

Clattering down to the bank of the pond
from the wet rocks – soil of the little island
turning underfoot, the tree-roots slick

with rain – and the light is only enough
to make out a few bats, a willow
leaning down to touch the water,

just enough to see how each thing
is altered. On my knees, I put my hand
into the dark of the pond, watch it open

like a white flower. Are we all
just wanting to see ourselves
changed, made unearthly? Tonight,

it seems like everything is trying
to get close to the water –
the willow, the hanging ash –

and as usual, on the opposite bank,
the night-fishermen are sitting
with their torches, lines held out,

waiting for a sign. Just now,
it starts to rain: I watch the pond
pock and sting – its sheet a patience

held for too long – and I, down
on my knees with the pond,
at eye-level with it, watch it breaking;

and the world is down on its knees
beside me – the sky, the rain shattering
its own image and mine. Once,

I queued for the baths
at the sanctuary at Lourdes, was sent
to a room full of frail men undressing:

just a damp white curtain between us
and the icy water rising up
from the Gave de Pau, the deep chant

of a Latin rosary, how a French voice
called to me. Two men inside, a crucifix
on the wall above the stone bath, my towel

taken off. I was given, instead, a sheet
of cotton to wrap around myself,
as though to reassure me that I could be loved

when all my parts were bound together.
All I can remember now is being held
(one hand on my chest, another pressed

to my back); the slow meeting of water
over my body, how the rhythm
of the voices and the river seemed

to reassemble my life around me.
And now the rain is smashing down
into the pond – this is it, I think:

I came here to see myself shattered
and remade, if only to show myself
that it is possible, and the moon

has turned my skin to silver,
and the willow with its head laid down
on the water is whispering something

in its sleep. I get up, pull myself
through the trees: snowberry,
hazels, thistles, bracken . . .

It is so black I can barely see myself
anymore – as I walk it is as though
I am leaving my body by the pond's

moonlit edge – and I wonder what creatures
will come to the water when I have left
(to drink, to feel themselves made whole

by drinking), will find me, will live
beyond my knowledge of them.
For now, the park is so black I am almost

swimming in it, and I only notice
how, from underneath, the trees are all
interlocking (the night-fishermen

casting out again, muttering) –
the night's focus, how everything
is reaching down into the earth

or into the water, each thing quietly
at its work, trying to bring some life
up to the surface, unharmed.

IN THE BODE-MUSEUM

On a narrow plinth in the corner
of the gallery, a stone portrait:
a man, his mouth unlipped

by fire, marble of the face
peeled off in the blaze. But the clothes
were spared somehow, as though

above the neck he was hung
on a noose of flame. And still
one unburnt eye, looking up

over the broken shoulder
to where his sculptor stood.
But hush. No one is coming.

We are handed our lives
by a fierce work. Onto which
blank space will I lock my gaze

when my father
is gone? How am I to wear
his love's burning mantle?

TWO REFLECTIONS

The dream splits its pod in the silence:
my father is standing, one midsummer,
in the park, surrounded by deer — a doe
and three fawns — and he is reaching up
on tiptoe, his right arm grasping into the lucid
liquid shimmer of the lime leaves,
pulling down young sprays in threshes
of green for the deer to eat. One fawn's furred
antlers are adorned with leaf; and its neck
longs for him. Eyes of deep marble,
the flank a constellation of stippled white.
From where I stand, it seems to swim
through the mirage, my father at the centre,
and even the memory is a picture held
on a pool — these souls alive in it, lush
in water. I stretch my hand to reach him
and they unshoal; a lost image, a dispersal.

A gurgled note – high and bubbling –
the moorhen busy with her nest, shimmying
into the pond, wearing her mask: the red petal
of the shield daubed over the skull, aureolin
armour of the beak-tip, and then I see them:
brown, speckled eggs in the intervals
of reed-light, leaf-chartreuse, and the nest
reflected in the water, perched on constant
motion. We cannot know the truth of water
before we know its touch, its break, the tendrils
of sun re-gathering. Never a stillness, the sky
split from water, the nest from the image
of the nest, and the bird sliding across,
picking twigs: an aerial shadow over the bed
of the pond. It is only where the darkness travels
that we picture depth, the silt and the truth of it.

TREE OF JESSE

Father, you would have loved
that frenzy of wood –
the sacred grove brought inside

and carved as though the heritage
of God was hidden in the branches
all along. I remember

stepping from the bright street
into the church, the sun
burning across my vision –

and on the north aisle, in shadow,
a body lying at the foot of a tree –
baroque splendour of wood,

the gilded vines curling roofwards
and on the branches twelve men
like gaudy fruits blooming

in the order of their lineage.
The body clasped at the root,
the tree lifting its blood

in ropes through the trunk, feeding,
and at the top the Christ-child
like the sun ringed

in hammered gold in the arms
of his mother. And now, standing
at your bedside, that tree

is a visitation – instead of Jesse,
it is you lying there – your body
proliferating upwards, being

reconstituted, broken down
into growth, and I cannot unsee it –
the corpse of my father, some message

of guilt at my own living.
For weeks now you have been
a rhythmic, breathing body –

hardly waking, chest
like a bellows, inflating, deflating –
mechanical, in and out –

the trachea ribbed and prominent
pulling the air. For so long
your breathing has lived

beyond your body. I woke last night
to imagine you were lying here
in my room. Total stillness

of the fields outside, at the window
the bronze gauze of the beech-leaves
pulsing in quiet shimmers – and me

bolt upright, startled to hear
that constant awful rattling
as though the air itself

was living. I called out
from my bed, but (what
was I expecting?) no reply.

Some nights, the sun fierce
at the window, I want to tell
my father to burn, to go down,

my forehead pressed
to his forehead, his shallow
breath in mine.

But the moon
(in the heavens God has pitched
a tent also for the moon) –

its ebbing shape, slivering out
and then sliding back into its bright
circle, its restless life.

Those who we love, and who die,
become gods to us. Our speech,
from that moment, is incantation.

We are heard beyond the world.
Now I think I can conjure you
when I am alone. I ask you

to place your hand on my shoulder
to steer me through.
This morning, I sang to you

as I carried the cup of tablets
through the sunlit house
like a celebrant. In your dream,

you told me, I was riding my bike
on the cinder path, my head-light
powering through the tunnel of trees –

and I felt in that moment
the privilege of being alive
in your mind, to have been remade

beyond myself and beamed out
in the flickering room of your sleep.
You are not leaving, I know,

but shifting into image – my head
already is haunted with you.
I have become a living afterlife.

All images return to you –
the body at the root
of my branching. And later,

a silver birch in the churchyard –
set apart from the mock orange,
its blowsy heads unpicking

their blossom in the wind,
almost a wedding – two plots down
from where you will be buried.

The skin of it scarred
with diamonds, catching
at dawn the pink fire of the sun,

and the body at its feet,
the white roots moving towards it
in the earth. May I always wake

on that image – the eastern pyre,
the bands of light and shadow ascending
the trunk until the birch-leaves flash

heaven-silvered on the underside
like a thousand doors, and know
that a soul is passing through.

TA PROHM

A stifling heat – the air heavy –
and all around the loud, wet forest
knotting the gaps in its own sound.

A peace long-earned, then broken;
and you, far off in the hospice bed.
Silk-cotton, strangler-fig

fastened here on the temple
as though it grew down from heaven,
was sent to hold in place

all this human work. And later,
through the house of fire, the fallen
galleries, I climbed in blue smoke

to where the god sat
ringed with incense. And yes,
I knelt to her. And yes, I prayed

through unbelief. Perhaps now,
father, only something old
and impossible can save us.

TONGUES OF FIRE

And up here, something uncanny
appearing through the drizzle –
a dozen or more junipers, all ranked

with bright tongues – yellow fruiting
thorns pricked in hundreds over the bark
like a sheath of fire, rot the colour

of the sun's late wheel slowing
over the brittle heath where,
in the grey damp of April,

some mute violence is budding
on all these shaking forms.
A fungus, blooming in orange horns –

and I would say that I have come upon
the cones of God, the Pentecostal flame
fallen to the bush at night

and burning here like a prophecy
that everything will be lit
before it is consumed. But now

I have learnt (as we all do, in time)
that no flesh is incorruptible –
which is why I am here

on the uplands with the goldcrest
and the firecrest nesting. *Clavariiforme* –
these tongues are rooted in the branch

and must ruin it to speak;
and so, I wonder, must God be known
through entropy? The matter of the world

dissolved, taken back
into the empty, inconceivable, ensouled
nothing that waits behind

and presses against its forms. God
like an intimacy that pressures
and bends; and this, today, is where

he has chosen to speak,
or where I have chosen to hear him speaking,
where I have conjured meaning

when I have needed
to see a fungus on the juniper
as a bright, ancestral messenger

bursting through from one realm
to another – a sign of what? An oracle
or a breaking of Christ in a reel

of telial horns, to give an account
of the world as it has changed for us.
Closer, it is almost as though I can hear

the bush ticking, the cells of the wood
dividing as the tongues
push out and lick the air

and soften their embers
on the bark. I hold out my hands –
wanting heat, some evidence

of energy releasing, a voice
to speak even in the friction
of atoms on the air, but nothing now,

nothing but the thrum
of the wind and the itch
of the branches rubbing their thin wrists

sore in the open.
Over all this wide heath
the spores are lifting, being

carried off and latching down
in the hedgerows where the haws
will come white and ruined –

the cancer's metastatic
flight from host to host through the air
as though I am living in it.

All this to say that, since the news,
we have leant around my father and known
love's fragility, its immanence

in the body, the proximity it takes
to material form – visible here on the heath
but at home unseen, working inward.

This morning, I knelt by his bed
and held his thin hand, my thumb
pressed around his, palms touching,

and kissed it while he slept.
Only the rattle of his chest lifting
and sinking (hardly any words

for weeks now – the tumour
suppressing the vocal chords)
and then a sudden need

to see inside, to know for myself
which cells on the lung were splitting
each minute and breaking time

into this kaleidoscope
of slow haul and frantic loss.
No apparition, no tongue of fire

to tell us before too late
of the blight on his frame, only
a few months and then this –

and so we hold him now
while he is here, listen to the organs
tell what they can of life, our insufficiency,

and we weigh it over with a spill
of love, an undyked river as if
now or never the world must be flooded

with its soul – knowing that as one body
breaks we must break our own
to show ourselves, to split

the God from us. And is this nature
turned outwards? This disruption –
is it a way of working, a way of nature

inverting so that God can be known?
Too cruel, surely – this is love working
against the world – this is when

we make God, and speak in his voice.
Crying, again, amongst the shivering wild.
Father, like God we can only talk

through things – a tongue of fire
lashing and nothing incorruptible.
Our life is a theophany –

we will work to know through time
what flesh can hold, the moment
in which a magnitude

can be carried inside a form
without it breaking. In this world, I believe,
there is nothing lost, only translated –

our lives are shot through it
and I am here this evening as a supplicant,
asking over and over

for correlation – that when all is done,
and we are laid down in the earth, we might
listen, and hear love spoken back to us.

NOTES & ACKNOWLEDGEMENTS

From *Buile Suibhne*. These poem-translations are indebted to J. G. O'Keefe's edition, translation and glossary of the middle-Irish tale *Buile Suibhne* (London: Alfred Nutt, 1913). The poems I have written are in part translations, and in other instances are lyric inventions or reworkings inspired by the original text.

Old Croghan Man. The torso and arms of 'Old Croghan Man', a preserved set of remains found in a bog near Croghan Hill, Co. Offaly, are held at the National Museum of Ireland, Dublin. The epigraph to this poem is taken from Eamonn P. Kelly, 'An Archaeological Interpretation of Irish Iron Age Bog Bodies', in Sarah Ralph, ed., *The Archaeology of Violence: Interdisciplinary Approaches* (Albany, NY: State University of New York Press, 2012), 232-40.

Vestige. The title of this poem refers to Robert Chambers's 1844 work *Vestiges of the Natural History of Creation*. The italicised text in the poem is taken from the diaries of Gerard Manley Hopkins. 12 February 1870 – 'The slate slabs of the urinals even are frosted in graceful sprays.' See *The Collected Works of Gerard Manley Hopkins*, Vol. III: Diaries, Journals & Notebooks, ed. Lesley Higgins (Oxford: Oxford University Press, 2015).

In the Bode-Museum. This poem refers throughout to a marble portrait of Acellino Salvago by the Italian Renaissance sculptor Antonio della Porta (better known as Tamagnino), held in the Bode-Museum, Berlin. The portrait was transferred to the Flak tower at Friedrichshain for safekeeping during the Second World War, but was heavily damaged by fire.

Tree of Jesse. The Tree of Jesse referenced in the poem is one of the baroque altarpieces at the Igreja de São Francisco, Porto, and was carved by Filipe da Silva and António Gomes in the early eighteenth century.

Thanks are due to the editors of the following magazines and anthologies in which some of these poems first appeared: *And Other Poems*, *IV Anthology*, *London Magazine*, *Magma*, *Manchester Review*, *New Statesman*, *Oxford Poetry*, *Poetry Ireland Review*, *Poetry Review*, *Resurgence & Ecologist*, *Rialto* and *Virginia Quarterly Review*.

A selection of these poems won a Northern Writers' Award in 2016. Thanks are also due to Arts Council England, for a Grant for the Arts in 2014, and to The Poetry Trust for an Aldeburgh Eight bursary in 2015. 'Ilex' was the winner of The Resurgence Prize in 2017. Some of these poems were originally published in *Lantern* (Offord Road Books, 2019), which was Poetry Book Society Summer Pamphlet Choice, 2019, and which won an Eric Gregory Award, 2019.

I would like to thank Robin Robertson, for his diligence and support in editing this manuscript; and Andrew McMillan, for his generosity, insight and friendship. 'Adoration' is for Nick. Thanks to Will, for letting me write some of these poems. And to others, too, who gave their time and energy to my earlier drafts: Sarah Hymas, Carola Luther, Okechukwu Nzelu, Ruby Robinson, Pauline Rowe, Martha Sprackland, Helen Tookey.

I would also like to thank my parents, for their unending support. The final poems here are dedicated, with love, admiration and gratitude, to the memory of my father, Paul Hewitt (1957-2019).